Asheville,
North Carolina through the Seasons

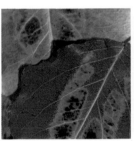

A PHOTOGRAPHIC PORTRAIT

First published in the United States
of America by:

Twin Lights Publishers, Inc.
10 Hale Street
Rockport, Massachusetts 01966
Telephone: (978) 546-7398
http://www.twinlightspub.com

and

Yourtown Books
Naples, Florida
Telephone: (941) 262-0716

ISBN 1-885435-36-3

10 9 8 7 6 5 4 3 2 1

Book design by
SYP Design & Production, Inc.
http://www.sypdesign.com

Cover Photo by: Bill Duyck
Back Cover Photos by: John E. Keys, Susan F. Quirk,
Steven Lamar Youngblood, and Melissa Jo Richart

Printed in China

Other titles in the Photographic Portrait series:

Cape Ann
Kittery to the Kennebunks
The Mystic Coast, Stonington to New London
The White Mountains
Boston's South Shore
Upper Cape Cod
The Rhode Island Coast
Greater Newburyport
Portsmouth and Coastal New Hampshire
Naples, Florida
Sarasota, Florida
The British Virgin Islands
Portland, Maine
Mid and Lower Cape Cod
The Berkshires
Boston
Camden, Maine
Sanibel and Captiva Islands
San Diego's North County Coast
Newport Beach, California
Phoenix and the Valley of the Sun
Wasatch Mountains, Utah
The Florida Keys
Miami and South Beach
Maryland's Eastern Shore
Charleston, South Carolina
Savannah, Georgia

ACKNOWLEDGMENT

Twin Lights Publishers & Yourtown Books wish to thank all of the photographers who submitted their work for our consideration. Because of space limitations, we were not able to include many excellent photographs in *Asheville, North Carolina Through the Seasons: A Photographic Portrait.*

We extend our thanks to the judges, Margaret Williams and Andrea Jackson, whose expertise has resulted in three winning photographs. They have selected photographs that describe the Asheville area beautifully.

Margaret Williams is a senior reporter/photographer for the *Mountain Xpress*, weekly newspaper in Asheville. Originally from the Gulf Coast of Alabama, she made Asheville her home more than ten years ago. In addition to writing, she has competed successfully at the national level in karate and now trains and teaches at the Center for Martial Arts.

Andrea Jackson, a photographer for the *Hendersonville Times*, is a recent graduate of UNCA with a degree in psychology and art. Andrea melds her interests through photography.

Allison Morris spent countless hours coordinating the photographic contest and the judging.

Tim Barnwell is a commercial and fine art photographer based in Asheville, NC. His career has spanned over twenty years as both photographer and photography instructor. For eight years, he served as executive director of the nationally recognized school, Appalachian Photographic Workshops. We are grateful to him for the use of aerial photographs.

The local photo and camera shops cooperation in sharing the contest information with their customers is appreciated. Special thanks go to the Buncombe County Library who most graciously hosted the judging of the contest. Also to The Biltmore Estate for providing courtesy photographs of the Estate and grounds, the Grove Park Inn for courtesy photographs of the Inn and grounds, and the Asheville Chamber of Commerce for courtesy photographs of the Asheville area.

We are grateful to Sarah FK Coble, who has written the captions for the photographs.

Finally, our thanks to Sara Day of SYP Design & Production, Inc., who has created another beautiful book.

contents

introduction

Asheville, North Carolina is a town with altitude. Cupped gently in a valley in the Appalachian Mountains, Asheville is the vibrant heart of Western North Carolina's mountain highlands and yet a world apart. Its distinctive Appalachian music and craft traditions, its funky urban atmosphere, and its gorgeous natural surroundings are a magnet for performing artists, writers, artisans, outdoor enthusiasts, natives of North Carolina and transplants from around the world of every age and from all walks of life.

It began as a mountain paradise. Shrouded in the mists of the formidable Blue Ridge and Great Smoky mountains, a small town originally known as "Eden Land" was a remote, hard to reach place settled largely by native American Indians and hardy Scotch-Irish farmers. Officially incorporated in 1797 as Asheville after North Carolina Governor, Samuel Ashe, the town remained in misty isolation in which a rich, unique culture grew and still thrives in the region's music and artistic traditions. Asheville and the surrounding areas play host to several world class music festivals throughout the year, including the Black Mountain Folk Festival, the North Carolina International Folk Festival, the Brevard Music Festival, and Asheville's Bele Chere Festival.

Artists, craftspeople and writers have also gravitated to the Asheville region to study and work either in the city's time-mellowed art deco-style downtown, or in the mountains' wooded cool and quiet. The area is home to more than a few famous and well-loved American writers and poets, such as historian/ poet, Carl Sandburg, novelist Thomas Wolfe, short story writer, O. Henry, as well as

contemporary authors, Charles Frazier, John Ehle, and Wilma Dykeman. The legendary F. Scott Fitzgerald also spent many summers languishing in Asheville.

Asheville's fortune has had as many peaks and valleys as the hills which surround it. But the hardy mountain spirit of its people and the town's beautiful natural surroundings are a tough combination to beat.

Asheville today is vibrant and progressive, both its new and old architecture and its spirits are restored to new life. Carefully nurturing its own unique history and artistic culture, Asheville reaches out to embrace the new. Surrounded by national parks and miles of mountain forests, it is a popular departing point for wilderness adventure, yet maintains its own quiet urban flair. Asheville is a small city, with a very large soul. As the local saying goes: altitude affects attitude.

Malcolm Glass' image of Asheville's beloved S&W Cafeteria looks as though it may have been taken with a fisheye lens. In fact, it was captured with a Russian-made Horizon panoramic camera on an afternoon of exploring Asheville with his photographer wife, Mitzi Cross. "I'm intrigued with the distortion of straight lined things like buildings. I have also shot some fairly weird close-up "panoramas" of nudes and hot rods. If you use one of those cameras that just crops the top and bottom fourth of a negative or if you stitch together a series of digital images you don't get the same effect. This thing has a lens that pans across the film and gives you a 35 mm negative, that's the standard width but about 2 1/2 times longer," Glass writes from his home in Clarksville, Tennessee, where he is a teacher of creative writing and photography.

Malcolm Glass, who is the author of several plays, including *Greetings, Sisters,* and *All Bets Off*, as well as numerous short stories and collections of poetry, began his affair with photography on a fellowship to Australia and Europe where "I shot of a lot of pretty good slides with a Petri Rangefinder that I got in a pawn shop for about $15." Glass and Cross are currently exploring the possibility of relocating to Asheville.

FIRST PRIZE

S&W Cafeteria and Environs

MALCOLM GLASS
HORIZON 202 PANORAMIC
TMAX
F16@1/250

Built around 1927 by Asheville's native architect Douglas Ellington, the S&W is an excellent specimen of the jazz age architecture of Asheville's boom years.

SECOND PRIZE

Craggy Gardens: Beauty That Makes Us Stand in Silence.

CATHRYN SHAFFER
NIKON N-80
KODAK
F8

Known for its spectacular wildflower blooms and vast displays of catawba rhododendron, the Craggies are Asheville's most dramatic vista.

Photographer Cathryn Shaffer draws much of her inspiration from her faith. The title of her image of Craggy Gardens, in fact, comes from the line of a favorite hymn: "It is your beauty, Lord, that makes us stand in silence." A native of Savannah, who moved to Asheville in 1983, Shaffer writes that she has always had "an eye for details that folks might tuck away; those views and memories often hidden in people's hearts. They may believe that no one has noticed what is so important and they're surprised when someone acknowledges it." Her love of photography, as she describes it, springs from that ability to capture the spontaneity of the moment; pulling moments of the soul to the surface and recording them visually in time.

Shaffer's photographs were also included in *Savannah, Georgia: A Photographic Portrait,* in which she won third place.

Third place winner, Paul F. Willard finds North Asheville's Saturday Tailgate Market refreshingly quaint and personal. His image of his eighty-five year old next-door neighbor, Lassie Woody and her abundant floral world is an affectionate regard for the rugged individuals of his adopted mountain home. "Lassie Woody is my gardening mentor. She works in her flower garden every day and has beautiful results that frequently stop traffic," he writes. "In this photograph, I like how strong her arms look—a testament to the work she does growing the flowers. I also like the clown effect of so many flowers coming out of her tiny Volkswagen at the market."

A part-time freelance photographer, Willard first took a sincere interest in photography while working as a wilderness ranger for the US Forest Service in Telluride, Colorado. He now lives in North Asheville, only a few hundred yards away from the North Asheville Tailgate Market with his wife, Julie, and their dog, Raleigh.

THIRD PRIZE

Lassie Woody

PAUL F. WILLARD
CANON EOS ELAN 7E
FUJI
F8

Lassie Woody offers bouquets of flowers from her mountain garden in North Asheville for the Saturday morning Tailgate market.

spring

Mustard Grass, Yancey County

NEIL HARRIS
NIKON F-28MM LENS
KODACOLOR
F16

A field of golden mustard grass colors
an early spring field on Bald Creek in
Yancey County, 25 miles north and
east of Asheville.

**Dogwoods on the Shores of
Beaver Lake**

PHOTO COURTESY OF ASHEVILLE
CHAMBER OF COMMERCE

Practically surrounded by national
forests and parks, Asheville is a haven
for nature lovers. Beaver Lake, just
north of Asheville is a pleasant natural
escape.

Mountain Laurel

VIRGINIA SENECHAL
NIKON FE2 W/ 55 MICRO
KODAK MAX 400
F11

The blooming of the mountain laurel,
Kalmia latifolia, an evergreen shrub
native to the Western Carolina Highlands, brings floods of visitors up to
watch the mountains blossom with
bowers of white and pink blooms.

Asheville Iris

ALYCE KASM PATRICK
PENTAX ZX-10
FUJI 200
AUTO

Large, velvet-petaled iris, sometimes affectionately known as *"poor man's orchids,"* bloom in an Asheville garden.

Cullasaja Falls *(opposite)*

CYNTHIA L. WALKER
PENTAX K1000
KODAK
F2

Tumbling 250 feet down the rugged Cullasaja River Gorge, these falls are a dramatic sight along the narrow, winding road southeast of Asheville near Highlands, North Carolina.

Red Barn, Green Hills

JOHN E. KEYS
NIKON FE2
FUJICHROME
F22

The landscape of the North Carolina mountains reveals itself at every twist and turn of the famous Blue Ridge Parkway, just east of Asheville. Conceived in 1935 as part of Roosevelt's New Deal, the Blue Ridge Parkway provided a link between the Shenandoah National Park in Virginia and the Great Smoky Mountains National Park. The project employed the talents of Stanley Abbot, a young, gifted landscape architect and hundreds of Italian stonemasons.

Cardinalis Cardinalis

BILL DUYCK
NIKON FE2
KODACHROME 64
F22

The state bird of North Carolina, a male cardinal, feeds its young in an urban nest in Asheville.

In Like a Lamb *(left)*

ALYCE KASM PATRICK
PENTAX ZX-10
ROYAL GOLD 200
AUTO

Sheepish regard at the Western North Carolina Nature Center. This "living museum" exhibits a wide array of indigenous wild animals as well as domestic farm animals.

Spring Tulips

PHOTO COURTESY OF
GROVE PARK INN RESORT

Built in 1913 with native stone blasted
from nearby Sunset Mountain, The
Grove Park Inn remains one of
Asheville's greatest landmarks.

Spring on the Blue Ridge Parkway

JOHN E. KEYS
NIKON FE2
FUJICHROME
F11

The best place for a scenic drive, the
Blue Ridge Parkway, sweeps to the east
and south of Asheville, winding into the
mountains between Waynesboro, Virginia
and Cherokee, North Carolina.

Rounding the Bend

ALEXANDRA MORRIS
CANON
FUJI

Western North Carolina's manufacturing industry keeps several railroads' freight services busy.

Douglas Falls, Coleman Boundary *(opposite)*

CYNTHIA L. WALKER
PENTAX K1000
KODAK
F8

High in the rugged Black Mountains northeast of Asheville, Douglas Falls cascades through virgin stands of oak, hemlock, poplar and pine trees.

Belle Cherie

SANDRA MARSICANO
CANON AE1
FUJI 400
F5.6

Chic boutiques and funky antique stores co-exist on Asheville's friendly, diverse urban streets.

Spring Tulips in the Walled Garden at Biltmore Estate *(opposite)*

PHOTO COURTESY OF
THE BILTMORE COMPANY

The magnificent park surrounding George Vanderbilt's 250-room chateâu was designed by the famed landscape architect, Frederick Law Olmsted. In April, the gardens are host to the month-long *Festival of Flowers*, which highlight not only the precise lines of the formal gardens, but also the wild-flower plantings as well as the exotic blooms that thrive in the elegant Conservatory.

Gargoyle at Grove Arcade

DARLENE THOMPSON
MINOLTA
FUJICHROME
F11

The Grove Arcade, which in fact was never finished, is a unique example of Asheville's art deco architecture. It served for many decades as the U.S. Meteorological Station.

Foggy Sunrise *(above)*

SUSAN F. QUIRK
CANON REBEL 2000
100 SLIDE
F5.6

Fog obscures the sunrise over the mountains east of Asheville.

Pack Square: Vance Monument, City Building and the Jackson Building *(left)*

SUSAN F. QUIRK
CANON REBEL 2000
AGFA 100 CHROME
F5.6

Asheville's civic buildings still represent symbolic anchors to Asheville's urban life.

High Noon *(opposite)*

SUSAN F. QUIRK
CANON REBEL 2000
KODAK ELITECHROME 100
AUTO

The Vance Monument, in the center of Pack Square, was erected in 1898 in memory of Zebulon Vance, the first governor of North Carolina and a native of Asheville.

Pack Place from College Street

SUSAN F. QUIRK
CANON REBEL 2000
100 SLIDE FILM
AUTO

The graceful tower of the Jackson Building anchors a row of old and new buildings on Pack Square, including the Asheville Art Museum, the Diana Wortham Theater, and the new Pack Place, a newly created cultural arts center.

Horse Head Fountain *(opposite)*

SUSAN F. QUIRK
CANON REBEL 2000
KODAK ELITECHROME 100
F5.6

Designed by North Carolina artist, Jim Barnhill, Asheville's little bronze girl bends to drink from a fountain on a corner of Pack Square. The horse head fountain is a replica of similar fountains that serviced horses stopping to rest in the square.

Café on the Square

SUSAN F. QUIRK
CANON REBEL 2000
AGFA 100 CHROME
F5.6

Asheville's mild weather and lively downtown sidewalks make it a popular city for al fresco dining.

Appalachian Spring with Dogwoods *(opposite)*

TIM BARNWELL
CANON F1 WITH 50MM LENS
FUJICHROME 100
F11

Mountain wisdom advises to watch for the blooming of the dogwood tree in cold spring weather, or "dogwood winter." The North Carolina state flower, the dogwood, thrives in Asheville's cool mountain climate.

Old Europe, New World (above)

KIRSTIN MCKEEL
CANON EOS 500
KODAK 200
AUTO

Chic and shady, diners wile away the pleasant afternoon at the Old Europe Café on Battery Park.

Double Decker Latte, Please (left)

SUSAN F. QUIRK
CANON REBEL 2000
AGFA 100 CHROME
F6.7

A retired double decker bus now serves as a café on Biltmore Avenue.

First Baptist Church (opposite)

KAREN SLAGLE
MINOLTA

A signature Asheville landmark, the dome of the First Baptist Church of Asheville was inspired by the dome of the great cathedral in Florence, Italy.

Fade (top)

KAREN SLAGLE
MINOLTA

The mountains fade beneath the canopy of a cotton candy sky as seen from the sunset deck of the Grove Park Inn.

Spring Night Over Asheville (bottom)

TIM BARNWELL
CANON F1 WITH 50MM LENS
FUJICHROME 100
F11

After the fiscal and moral devastation of the Great Depression, Asheville stirred to new life in the 1940's, a renewal that continued with characteristic persistence and determination. The largest city west of the Blue Ridge Mountains, Asheville is a vital example of a progressive community that builds upon its history.

Nectar (opposite)

ALYCE KASM PATRICK
PENTAX 2X-10
KODAK ROYAL GOLD 200

A bee mines nectar in a pea flower.

Ah, Grasshopper

BILL DUYCK
NIKON FE2
KODACHROME 64
F22

A female eastern bluebird feeds her brood inside a nest cavity. Native to the southeastern U.S., nesting bluebirds are harbingers of spring to the Carolina Mountains around Asheville.

Mountain Mushroom

DIANE STRICKLAND

The loamy soil of the mountains and the cool damp air provide perfect conditions for around 2,000 varieties of mushrooms.

Azaleas *(opposite)*

DONALD B. SCHALLER
NIKON N70
FUJI 200
F5.6

A brilliant display of azaleas sets a
serene woodland ablaze with color at
the Biltmore Estate.

Duck Pond on Beaver Dam Road

BONNIE S. COOPER
NIKON
FUJI
F7-16

A brood of ducks have a rest period
on the shores of a duck pond off
Beaver Dam Road north of downtown
Asheville.

summer

Falls

R. ANDREW WYATT
MINOLTA
KODAK GOLD
F22

Hundreds upon hundreds of waterfalls
fill the mountains of Western North
Carolina with their misty music, from
the majestic roar of a Bridal Veil
cataract, to a delicate trickle of water
tripping down mossy stones.

Jackson Building from Market Street *(opposite)*

SUSAN F. QUIRK
CANON REBEL 2000
KODAK ELITECHROME 100
F4

Asheville's first "skyscraper," the graceful spire of the Jackson Building was erected on the site of author Thomas Wolfe's father's tombstone business.

St. Lawrence Basilica

DARLENE THOMPSON
MINOLTA
FUJICHROME
F16

Designed by architect Rafael Gustavino, who also worked on the Biltmore House, the St. Lawrence Basilica has the largest Catholic congregation in Western North Carolina.

Biltmore Estate

PHOTO COURTESY OF
THE BILTMORE COMPANY

After travelling to Asheville with his mother in 1888, George Vanderbilt, grandson of shipping and railroad magnate Cornelius Vanderbilt, fell in love with the natural beauty of the Carolina Mountains. Originally consisting of 125,000 acres, Biltmore Estate now covers 8,000 acres. The 250-room Biltmore House remains the largest private residence in the country.

Boatman on Beaver Lake *(opposite)*

DARLENE THOMPSON
MINOLTA
FUJICHROME
F16

A lone boater enjoys the summer sunset on Beaver Lake, north of Asheville.

Market Street: Asheville Supply and Foundry *(above)*

SUSAN F. QUIRK
CANON REBEL 2000
AGFA
F7

Evidence of Asheville's adaptability, Market Street's rich architecture has housed businesses ranging from the nuts and bolts of machinery to newer businesses, including gourmet chocolates, mountain real estate, and art studios and galleries.

City Building from The Vance Monument *(left)*

SUSAN F. QUIRK
CANON REBEL 2000
AGFA 100 CHROME
F5.6

Designed by Asheville native Douglas Ellington, City Hall, with its distinctive pink tiled roof, is one of Asheville's most memorable landmarks. Pack Square, and the County Plaza are regular sites for the city's beloved festivals, including the *Bele Chere Festival* and the summer-long *Shindig on the Green*.

Pillars

AARON HOGSED
FUJI GSW690
FUJI PROVIA

The ornate, gothic façade of the Jackson Building and neighboring structures are beacons of another time.

Pack Square: Municipal Building, Jackson Building, Legal Building

SUSAN F. QUIRK
CANON REBEL 2000

After the hey days of the Roaring '20's, Asheville fell hard into the Great Depression as its luxury based economy evaporated and left the city under crushing debt. Much of Asheville's rich architectural heritage survives because for fifty years, the city was simply too poor to tear it down.

Light Post Garden at North Carolina Arboretum

SUSAN F. QUIRK
CANON REBEL 2000
AGFA RSX 11
F6.7

The North Carolina Arboretum has several showcase gardens within the 6,300 acre confines of the Bent Creek Experimental Forest, and surrounded by the Pisgah National Forest including a Quilt Garden, a Spring Garden, and the Plants of Promise Garden.

Biltmore Building (opposite)

AARON HOGSED
FUJI GSW690
FUJI PROVIA

Internationally renown architect I. M. Pei's sleek lines and rippling expanses of glass in Pack Square reflect Asheville's rich architectural fabric.

Scenic Overlook

KAREN SLAGLE
MINOLTA

A scenic overlook from the legendary
Blue Ridge Parkway shows the sweeping fertile valleys and the dense,
swaths of clouds that have earned
them the title "Smoky Mountains."

Obelisk, Pack Square (opposite)

EDGAR C. HARRIS
PENTAX K-1000
FUJI PROVIA
F16

Funds to build the obelisk of the Vance
Monument were provided by George
Willis Pack, after whom Asheville's
central square is named.

Mellow Mushroom and Antique Shop

SUSAN F. QUIRK
CANON REBEL 2000
KODAK ELITECHROME 100
F5.6

A quirky eatery which began in Atlanta and is now famous in the southeast, the Mellow Mushroom, is an instantly recognizable downtown hangout with Asheville's young pizza lovers.

Playbills

SANDRA MARSICANO
CANON AE1
FUJI 400
F5.6

Cluttered playbills on a downtown post advertise Asheville's young, vibrant urban cultural scene.

Hogan's Watch Repair

SANDRA MARSICANO
CANON AE1
FUJI 400
F8

The busy window of a homey, downtown shop brings Mayberry to mind.

UNC-Asheville Botanical Garden

MICHAEL L. PEAVLER
MINOLTA X 700
FUJI VELVIA
F16

Dedicated to the preservation of native
Appalachian flora, the Botanical
Gardens of University of North
Carolina, Asheville were begun in
1960 by the Asheville Garden Club
and designed by nationally acclaimed
landscape artist, Doan Ogden.

Art for Art's Sake *(opposite)*

SANDRA MARSICANO
CANON AE1
KODAK 400
F8

A quirky metal sculpture entitled
"Shopping Daze" stands on the side-
walk outside of Malaprop's Bookstore,
an Asheville tradition and the heart of
the city's vibrant arts and letters life.
The sculpture was installed by the
Asheville Downtown Association, and
was created by Tekla, Dan Howachyn
and Black Mountain Iron Works.

Mountain Air, Chinese Lanterns (above)

ALICE HARRIS
CANON EOS 750
FUJI 400

The Noodle Shop is one among an eclectic variety of cafes, bistros and ethnic restaurants that line Asheville's lively summer sidewalks.

Food Lion Skate Park (left)

MICHELE HIESTAND
CANON A-1
VELVIA
F22

After a ban on skateboarding around Pack Square and on the Vance Monuments, Asheville's boarders got a home of their own on the corner of Flint and Cherry Streets in downtown Asheville.

Jackson Building (opposite)

MITZI M. CROSS
MAMIYA 645
ILFORD 120 DELTA 100
F11

The ornate Jackson Building stands like a beacon on the edge of Asheville's Pack Square. Pack Square is a village green that still anchors Asheville's youthful and lively downtown.

Grove Park Inn

PHOTO COURTESY OF
GROVE PARK INN RESORT

Considered a marvel of modern engi-
neering when it was built in the early
20th century, the Grove Park Inn's arts
and crafts style furnishings and
appointments are carefully and consis-
tently maintained.

Red Roofs, Green Mountains

Tonic tycoon, Edwin Wiley Grove's vision of an inn of "home-like and wholesome simplicity," became manifest in the rough hewn stone building of this famous Asheville inn. The 142 room resort was built in just over one year, with the work of 400 builders, stonemasons, and laborers.

Tailgate Produce Market *(opposite)*

PAUL F. WILLARD
CANON EOS ELAN 7E
FUJI
F8

Gardeners from all around Asheville congregate on Saturdays at the Tailgate Produce Market in North Asheville. A popular stop for locals and visitors alike, it is a place to pick up fresh herbs, produce, gossip, and sometimes a few stale jokes.

Rose Garden

PHOTO COURTESY OF
THE BILTMORE COMPANY

The Walled Garden is four acres total; of that, part is planted with 2,300 rose bushes.

Twilight

PHOTO COURTESY OF ASHEVILLE
CONVENTION AND VISITORS' BUREAU

The lights of Asheville wink on as summer's lavender twilight settles over the Blue Ridge Mountains.

Nicotiana

NEIL HARRIS
NIKON OS-35 MM LENS
FUJICHROME
F16/125

Flowering tobacco plants scent the summer air in Jack's Creek, Yancey County, northwest of Asheville.

Hum

CHERYL W. LEWIS
NIKON N70
KODAK MAX 200

Perhaps this hummingbird, common
in the Carolina Mountains, can't
remember the words to the song he's
humming as he hangs in midair, con-
templating the nectar-filled blooms of
a butterfly bush.

Contemplation *(opposite)*

KAREN SLAGLE
MINOLTA

Cradled in the 495,979 acre Pisgah
National Forest, known as the cradle of
American Forestry, the 426-acre
Western North Carolina Arboretum is
surrounded by one of the nation's
most beautiful natural settings.

UNC-Asheville Campus

TIM BARNWELL
CANON F1 WITH 50MM LENS
FUJICHROME 100
F8

Described by the prestigious *Fiske Guide to Colleges* as a "...public liberal arts university that offers...rigorous academics, small classes, and a beautiful setting," University of North Carolina Asheville was recognized among "the best and most interesting colleges in America" for the 8th consecutive year in 2002.

Shaconage

RICK AMMONS
NIKON F90X
FUJI VELVIA
F22

Early morning mist fills a valley near the Blue Ridge Parkway. The first European explorers to the North Carolina Highlands found the Cherokee Indians living in "Shaconage," or "Land of the Blue Mists."

Basilica of St. Lawrence: The Mother Church of Western North Carolina *(opposite)*

JOY MARIE FALK
NIKON FM-10
KODAK 200
F11

The term Basilica is a special designation by the pope to churches for their antiquity, dignity or historical significance as a center of worship. Barcelona-born architect, Rafael Guastavino, who designed Asheville's venerable Basilica of St. Lawrence, is also widely credited for the revival of an ancient Spanish tile and mortar system that uses layers of thin tile and mortar to create curved horizontal surfaces such as vaults or domes, a system which he employed throughout the Basilica.

Sunsets of Madison County *(above)*

KAREN L. STITELER
OLYMPUS STYLUS
KODAK 400
AUTO

This rugged country just northwest of Asheville is still much the same as it was at the turn of the last century. Forty-eight percent of the population still lives on farms, the highest percentage in the state.

Seeing Red *(right)*

ALEXANDRA MORRIS
CANON
KODAK

Fourth of July fireworks explode over the S&W Cafeteria on the corner of Haywood and Battery Park.

Red

ALYCE KASM PATRICK
PENTAX ZX-10
ROYAL GOLD 200
AUTO

An extreme close up of a rooster on
Farm Day at The Western North Carolina
Nature Center. Featuring exhibits such
as animal identification, weather fore-
casting, bee-keeping, as well as archae-
ological and zoological displays, the
Western North Carolina Nature Center
immerses visitors in natural history as
well as a peek into rural mountain life.

Sandburg's Farm

ALYCE KASM PATRICK
PENTAX 2X-10
KODAK ROYAL 100
AUTO

Pulitzer prize winning author and poet,
Carl Sandburg moved to the 240-acre
Connemara Farm near Hendersonville,
North Carolina in 1945. He lived there
happily for the last 22 years of his life
with his wife, three daughters, grand-
children and his wife's 200 prize dairy
goats.

Settlers

JOSEPH A. CORRIVEAU
PENTAX K1000

In the mid 18th century, German and Scottish immigrants pushed up the Great Wagon Road into the Carolina Mountains, seeking fertile valley farm land, pushing the Cherokee farther up into the mountains. In 1828, when gold was discovered in the mountains of Georgia, under pressure from prospectors and white settlers, President Andrew Jackson signed the Removal Act, which condemned all Eastern Native American tribes to a tragic march to the Oklahoma territory.

autumn

Colors Over the Falls of Graveyard Fields

BILL DUYCK
NIKON FE2
KODACHROME 25
F22

In 1925, fire devastated 25,000 acres of heavily logged forest in this area south of Asheville. The decimated valley, littered with blackened stumps resembled an ancient graveyard, which inspired the name. Three splendid waterfalls along the small Yellowstone Prong stream make this area a favorite among hikers and backpackers.

Sugar Maple, Graveyard Fields *(opposite)*

BILL DUYCK
NIKON FE2
KODACHROME 25
F22

The Yellowstone Prong, which got its name from the golden color of lichens and mineral deposits on the stream's rocks, runs along Graveyard Field's pretty, narrow valley. The Carolina Highland's high precipitation, mountain soil, and history of heavy logging and fire have produced a unique blend of trees and other vegetation.

Path

MICHELE HIESTAND
CANON A1
VELVIA
F22

A winding path is tracked with late afternoon shadows at the Botanical Gardens in Asheville.

Highland Park, Montford

MICHELE HIESTAND
CANON A-1
VELVIA
F16

Montford was developed as a pleasant
suburb for Asheville's upper middle
class citizens: doctors, lawyers, and
architects built homes in this progres-
sively designed village, which was
annexed to the city of Asheville in 1905.

Fall Color, Black Mountains

NEIL HARRIS
NIKON F
FUJICHROME
F16

Blazing reds and oranges on the Mount Mitchell Golf Course in Yancey County shows up in brilliant contrast to the green of the Black Mountains in the distance.

Grove Park Inn in Autumn

PHOTO COURTESY OF
GROVE PARK INN RESORT

A cozy place to take shelter from the chilly autumn rains, the historic Grove Park Inn Resort still offers spectacular vistas of autumn foliage.

Linville Gorge from Wiseman's View *(opposite)*

BILL DUYCK
NIKON FE2
KODACHROME 64
F22

One of the most rugged and wildly beautiful places in the country, the Linville Gorge's 7,600 acres of wilderness rise and fall precipitously more than a thousand feet up from the river bed.

Lagoon *(above)*

PHOTO COURTESY OF
THE BILTMORE COMPANY

On autumn weekends, Biltmore
Estate commemorates the unique
blend of ancient English customs
with Southern Appalachian traditions in an event called *Michaelmas:
An English Harvest Fair.*

Biltmore Estate Autumn *(left)*

PHOTO COURTESY OF
THE BILTMORE COMPANY

Although famous for its spectacular springtime *Festival of Flowers*,
the remaining carefully landscaped
and maintained 8,000 acres of
Biltmore Estate are ablaze with
fall color.

French Broad River

SUSAN F. QUIRK
CANON REBEL 2000
AGFA 50
F5.6

Famous among rafting enthusiasts for its whitewaters, the French Broad River tumbles through the 80,000 acre French Broad Ranger District just east of Asheville before spilling into Tennessee. The settlement and development of Asheville and surrounding areas primarily sprang up around this wide river, whose name was begotten not from lonely mountain men dreaming of Parisian ladies, but for the fact that it flowed in the direction of French held territories.

Gazebo and Gold: French Broad River Park *(opposite)*

SUSAN F. QUIRK
CANON REBEL 2000
AGFA 50
F5.6

One of the world's most ancient rivers, the French Broad River, was known by the Cherokees as "the Long Man," and its many forks and sidestreams were called "Chattering Children." French Broad River Park is located at a deep bend in the river, where it is joined by the waters of the Swannanoa River.

Mt. Pisgah Sunset

JOHN E. KEYS
NIKON FE2
KODACHROME
F8

The highest peak on Asheville's horizon, Mount Pisgah, southeast of the city, is the source of some debate among outdoor enthusiasts. While often identified as part of the Pisgah Mountains or Pisgah Ledge, the peak is also claimed as part of the Great Balsam Mountains. Pisgah took its name from the legendary mountain from which Moses was allowed to see the Promised Land.

Riverside Cemetery

SUSAN F. QUIRK
CANON REBEL 2000
FUJI SENSIA 200
F5.6

Asheville's Riverside Cemetery is located just northeast of downtown in the historic Montford District. Many of Asheville's famous residents are buried in this beautifully landscaped park, including authors Thomas Wolfe and William "O. Henry" Porter, North Carolina Governor, Zebulon Vance, as well as Confederate Brigadier Generals Thomas L. Clingman, and Robert B. Vance.

Wright Inn, Montford *(above)*

SUSAN F. QUIRK
CANON REBEL 2000
FUJI SENSIA 200
F5.6

Located in the Montford District, the historic Wright Inn, built in 1899 at the height of Asheville's boom years, is a fine example of Queen Anne style architecture. Originally built as a private home for Osella and Leva Wright and nicknamed "Faded Glory" by Ashevillians, the old house, lovingly restored into a quaint bed and breakfast is on the National Historic Register.

Katherine's Bed and Breakfast, Montford *(right)*

SUSAN F. QUIRK
CANON REBEL 2000
FUJI SENSIA 200
F5.6

In the era between 1870 and the 1930's, Asheville enjoyed a great prosperity as a resort town. Many elegant homes sprang up along the tree-lined streets of the Montford District for doctors, lawyers and architects who worked in the city. These solid, finely built homes survive today, often carefully renovated into homey bed and breakfasts.

Fire on the Mountain

RALSTON FOX SMITH
NIKON F3 HP
FUJI VELVIA

The evening light illuminates the
autumn-kissed leaves of maple
and chestnut on a hillside north
of Asheville.

Mums

CATHRYN SHAFFER
NIKON N-80
KODAK GOLD 200
F8

A young child sits among the mums at the Great Pumpkin Sale at Abernethy United Methodist Church in West Asheville.

Medical Office, Highland Park, Montford *(above)*

CATHRYN SHAFFER
NIKON N-80
KODAK GOLD 200
F11

Although Montford was primarily a residential district, it was initially created as a separate and distinct village unto itself. Many doctors had their practices here, as well as other professional offices. At the northern end of Montford Avenue was the old Highland Hospital, whose patients included F. Scott Fitzgerald's wife Zelda, who died during a fire there in 1948.

Fall

CATHRYN SHAFFER
NIKON N-80
KODAK GOLD 200
F8

Riverside Cemetery's 87 acres were designated as a Buncombe County Treasure Tree Preserve in April of 1997.

Reading the Signs

BONNIE S. COOPER
NIKON 6006
FUJI
F16

According to old Cherokee myth, trees turn color and lose their leaves as the result of the inability to stay awake for seven days and seven nights to gain spirit power. Only the cedar, spruce, pine and holly were able to complete the vigil and as their reward, were granted the power to stay green throughout the winter.

Autumn at Beaver Lake *(top)*

KAREN L. STITELER
OLYMPUS STYLUS
KODAK 200
AUTO

In 1921, the damming of Beaverdam Creek created Beaver Lake at Baird Bottoms, just north of Asheville. The area, known as Lakeview Park became a popular neighborhood for Asheville's well-to-do, with many stately mansions built around this scenic lake.

Beaver Lake in Early Spring *(bottom)*

ALYCE KASM PATRICK
PENTAX ZX-10
KODAK GOLD 400
AUTO

Voted by *Mountain Xpress* as the number one dog walking locale in Asheville, Beaver Lake is also home to The Elisha Mitchell chapter of the National Audubon Society's Beaver Lake Bird Sanctuary, where several pairs of rare warblers have been spotted nesting in the past few seasons.

Tobacco Drying

DONALD B. SCHALLER
NIKON N70
FUJI 200
F5.6

Burley tobacco hangs out to dry in an open air shed on a Western North Carolina Farm. It was the rapid growth of the tobacco industry in the latter half of the 19th century that helped pull North Carolina out of its post-civil war devastation. Tobacco is raised in over 90% of the North Carolina counties, and the tobacco industry has historically provided as many as 1 in every 11 available jobs. However, most tobacco growers work farms less than 300 acres.

Montford Avenue

CATHRYN SHAFFER
NIKON N-80
KODAK GOLD 200
F11

Often called a "Victorian Neighborhood," the architects of Montford were, in fact, greatly influenced by a number of progressive, cosmopolitan design trends of the late 19th and 20th century.

Near Highland Park

CATHRYN SHAFFER
NIKON N-80
KODAK GOLD 200
F8

Many of the designs for the splendid homes in the Montford area can be traced directly back to Richard Sharpe Smith, who made his name as the supervising architect on the Biltmore House.

Fall Morning on Cee Cee's Farm Road, Yancey County *(opposite)*

KAY W. HARRIS
OLYMPUS STYLUS
KODACOLOR
AUTOMATIC

Temperate in climate, lushly wooded, with wide, sweeping valleys and the highest peaks east of the Mississippi, Yancey County is becoming a favorite escape for autumn visitors.

**Groceries, Sundries,
Tobacco** *(above)*

CATHRYN SHAFFER
NIKON N-80
KODAK GOLD 200
F8

A dilapidated general store on the corner
of Starnes and Flint in Montford sags
under the weight of autumn nostalgia.

**House on Cumberland Avenue,
Montford** *(left)*

CATHRYN SHAFFER
NIKON N-80
KODAK GOLD 200
F11

A large portion of Asheville's Montford
district was designated as an historic
district and listed on the National
Register of Historic Places in 1977.

Small City, Big Soul

TIM BARNWELL
CANON F1 WITH 50MM LENS
FUJICHROME 100
F8

Wilma Dykeman described the first
Scot-Irish settlers of the Asheville
region in *The French Broad:* "...espe-
cially strong in wanderlust and sense
of individuality." Asheville still embod-
ies that spirit in the 21st century.

House on Flint Street, Montford

CATHRYN SHAFFER
NIKON N-80
KODAK GOLD 200
F5.6

The small village of Montford, an area one mile north of Battery Park Hill, was incorporated in 1893, at the beginning of Asheville's boom years. The enterprise of developing the area was begun by the Asheville Loan, Construction and Improvement Company, but was later taken over by George Willis Pack, of Pack Square fame, a Midwesterner who moved to Asheville looking for business opportunities in 1885.

Bent Creek Bend

CATHRYN SHAFFER
NIKON N-80

With steep climbs, hard-packed level runs, and plenty of mud and scenic water hazards, the Bent Creek watershed, located in the Pisgah Ranger District of the Pisgah National Forest, is popular among the mountain biking set.

River Bend, Avery County (opposite)

NEIL HARRIS
NIKON F 28 MM LENS
KODACOLOR
F16

High in the Black Mountains, northwest of Asheville, this rugged rural county is home to the Southeast's highest ski slopes, great golf courses, and is also host to the now famous annual *Woolly Worm Festival.* Woolly worms' stripes are carefully analyzed to predict the severity of the coming winter.

West Asheville *(top)*

CATHRYN SHAFFER
NIKON N-80
KODAK 200
F8

West and East sections of Asheville are divided roughly by the French Broad River and one of its many forks.

Sulfur Cosmos *(bottom)*

CAREY BLONDIN
PENTAX
F8

In 1985, North Carolina's First Lady, Dorothy Martin encouraged the state's Roadside Environmental Unit to cultivate wildflowers along the highways and byways. The North Carolina Roadside Wildflower Program is a wild success, with over 3,000 acres of marigolds, dame's rockets, poppies, and sulfur cosmos from late spring until first frost.

Autumn Skyline

TIM BARNWELL
CANON F1 WITH 50MM LENS
FUJICHROME 100
F16

Asheville officially became the cultural and economic center of Western North Carolina when the first train rumbled through the Blue Ridge Swannanoa Tunnel in the Autumn of 1880.

Miles Building with Flat Iron *(above)*

MALCOLM GLASS
HORIZON 202 PANORAMIC
TMAX
F16@1/125

Created by Asheville artist, Reed Todd, this sculpture of a turn of the century flat iron is actually a visual pun on the nearby, distinctively shaped Flat Iron Building. Asheville's historic downtown was largely built in the boom years of the 1920's, and has more classic art-deco style buildings than any other city in the Southeast after Miami Beach.

Great Who? *(left)*

RICK AMMONS
NIKON F90X
FUJI PROVIA 100F

Little General, a great horned owl at the Western North Carolina Nature Center, takes an extremely close look. According to old mountain folk legend, the owl can foretell any number of events. If an owl hoots on the east side of a mountain, mountain wisdom holds, bad weather is certain to follow.

Sweeping Expanse

ELAINE AARON
CANON SLR
FUJI VELVIA SLIDE
F11

According to the lore of Native Americans in the North Carolina Mountains, the great mountains and valleys were formed by a great eagle who pushed and pulled the soft crust of the new earth with the movement of his powerful sweeping wings.

Terra Cotta

STEVEN LAMAR YOUNGBLOOD
PENTEX K1000
KODAK
F5.6

The elaborate terracotta ornament on
the old Grove Arcade faces a new
lease on life. Undergoing a $12 million
restoration, the building, which was
originally intended to be an indoor city
with shops, apartments and offices but
was never completed, will fulfill its
original intent.

Late Fawn

RICK AMMONS
NIKON F90X
FUJI PROVIA 100

An apparently late-born, one week old fawn finds refuge in the Western North Carolina Nature Center.

Recess: Sand Hill-Venable Elementary School

CATHRYN SHAFFER
NIKON N-80
KODAK GOLD 200
F8

Asheville's natural beauty, cultural diversity, high standard of education and its high quality of life attracts increasing numbers of young families from all over the country.

Mist Shrouded Horizon

RICHARD KING
RICOH
400 FUJI

The famous short story writer, William Sidney Porter (AKA O. Henry), who married an Asheville girl, was one of the few that could look on Asheville's dreamy, mist-shrouded horizon and not be awed. "I could look at these mountains a hundred years and not get an inspiration—they depress me," he wrote. However, after his death in New York City in 1910, he now rests eternally in Asheville's Riverside Cemetery.

Bridge at the Botanical Gardens (opposite)

ALYCE KASM PATRICK
PENTAX ZX-10
KODAK GOLD 100
AUTO

A mere 10 acres can mean a world of difference. The University of North Carolina at Asheville's 10 acre Botanical Gardens, are located right in the middle of north Asheville, yet the tiny, cold creek and bridge under the late autumn skeletons of trees seem to belong to another place and time.

Low Hanging Fruit

CATHRYN SHAFFER
OLYMPUS IS-3
KODAK 200
F11

It was the Scots, British and German
settlers that brought apple trees to the
North Carolina Highlands. This view
from one of the orchards at Sky Top
Orchard in Flat Rock is perched at the
top of Mt. McAlpine at 3,000 feet.

Field Trip

CATHRYN SHAFFER
NIKON N-80
KODAK 200
F8

Warm days and cool nights of Western
North Carolina summers create perfect
conditions for growing apples. It seems
no one wants to be indoors on the
crisp autumn days that mean apple
picking, pressed cider, hayrides and
fall picnics.

Fall Apples

CATHRYN SHAFFER
NIKON N-80

North Carolina's Central Mountains, which surround Asheville, are definitely Apple Country. Henderson County is the state's foremost producer of apples and its *Annual Apple Festival* has been the area's biggest event for almost 50 years.

winter

**After the Fall: Bridal Veil Falls
in Winter**

BILL DUYCK
NIKON FE2
KODACHROME
F22

Cascading 120 feet above the roadway
that winds through the Nantahala
Forest west of Asheville, Bridal Veil
Falls can be caught in suspended ani-
mation in a winter cold snap.

Otus

BILL DUYCK
NIKON FE2
KODACHROME 64
F22

A year round resident of the wood-
lands of the Carolina Highlands, a
rufus eastern screech-owl, (*Otus asio*)
makes himself cozy in a winter nest.

New Day

ALYCE KASM PATRICK
PENTAX ZX-10
KODAK ROYAL 100
AUTO

In 1899, Congress chartered the 56,000-acre Qualla Boundary, the Eastern Cherokee Reservation in Cherokee, about an hour west of Asheville. Eleven thousand descendants of the original tribe have returned to live in their homeland.

Ice Age

BILL DUYCK
NIKON FE2
KODACHROME 25
F22

Roan Mountain's threatened spruce fir forests are a legacy of the Ice Age, and support a unique ecosystem that includes rare indigenous plant and animal species as well as northern species that do not occur in the Southeastern U.S. except on high, cold plateaus such as those on Roan Mountain.

Cold Iron

DARLENE THOMPSON
MINOLTA
FUJICHROME
F11

Did you ever wonder if your tongue would stick if you put it on a cold iron? In Asheville's cold winter weather, Reed Todd's giant replica of irons used at the old local laundry beckons people to stick their tongues out…

Cold Mountain

BILL DUYCK
NIKON FE2
KODACHROME 25
F22

Winter on Roan Mountain, elevation 6,436 feet above sea level, 15 degrees below zero. Receiving around 100 inches of snow every winter and buffeted by high winds, the Black Mountains that surround Roan Mountain are an anomaly in the otherwise mild temperatures of the Southeastern mountains.

Sing We Noel

PHOTO COURTESY OF ASHEVILLE
CHAMBER OF COMMERCE

Carolers sing by candlelight at the
Light Up Your Holidays celebration.
Along with the summer *Bele Chere
Festival,* the weeks-long *Light Up*
celebration has played a merry part in
Asheville's revitalization. Parades, craft
fairs, tree festivals, and a myriad of
cultural events and performances for
all religious denominations unite the
city under a glow of holiday good will.

Winter Sunset *(opposite)*

BILL DUYCK
NIKON F2AS
KODACHROME 25
F22

Brilliant red winter sunset over the
confluence of the French Broad and
the Swannanoa Rivers. This conver-
gence, at the intersections of Meadow
Road, Amboy Road and Lyman Street
is an ideal place to take a winter hike.

Contemporary Dance *(above)*

ALVIN BABICH
YASHICA 6TN RANGEFINDER
EKTACHROME 100
F4

A class in contemporary dance at the Fletcher School of Dance in Asheville keeps balance. This 50 year old Asheville Institution's professional company, Land of the Sky Civic Ballet, produces its own well-received, unique rendition of *The Nutcracker* during every holiday season.

Independent Asheville *(left)*

LIS ANNA
KODAK 200
F4

An extra on the set during filming of a production on Carolina Lane in downtown Asheville. The city's growing, young, diverse population make Asheville one of the most artistically dynamic places in the Southeast.

George Vanderbilt's Library

PHOTO COURTESY OF
THE BILTMORE COMPANY

Although the library at Biltmore House stretches the meaning of "cozy," it is still a place where George Vanderbilt's guests enjoyed a quiet moment after exploring the estate. The Library contains 10,000 volumes, some dating from the year 1561, and the prodigious marble fireplace can accommodate a good blaze.

Sunset in the Land of the Sky *(opposite)*

KAREN SLAGLE
MINOLTA

It was the winter of 1829 when Andrew Jackson, defying a Supreme Court ruling, forced the Cherokee Indians to walk the 1,200 wintry miles west to the Oklahoma territory. On that Trail of Tears, thousands—nearly one third of the entire Cherokee nation—died of exposure, disease and exhaustion.

Light Up the Holidays

PHOTO COURTESY OF ASHEVILLE CHAMBER OF COMMERCE

Fireworks light Asheville's City Hall during *Light Up Your Holidays*, finishing up the city's sixteen year holiday tradition with a bang.

Moore's Cove Falls, Winter Music

BONNIE S. COOPER
NIKON
FUJI
F22

Not quite frozen, Moore's Cove Falls, in Transylvania County still trickles past the sheets of suspended ice that cling to the ledges. Nicknamed "The Land of Waterfalls," Transylvania County's hills are alive with the sound of music of more than 150 waterfalls.

Snowy Hedges/Warm Welcome *(top)*

ALYCE KASM PATRICK
PENTAX ZX-10
KODAK ROYAL 100

Snow is slow to clear in Asheville. Western North Carolina's winters are generally mild, but mountain snows have given rise to a number of ski resorts.

Peacock *(bottom)*

KIRSTIN MCKEEL
CANON EOS 500
KODAK 200
AUTO

A cold peacock surveys his wintry kingdom of the Western North Carolina Nature Center.

Meet Jack Frost

ALYCE KASM PATRICK
PENTAX ZX-10
KODAK MAX 400
AUTO

A mother introduces her young son to the wonders of snow.

Snow Day

CATHRYN SHAFFER
NIKON N-80
KODAK 400
F5.6

Kids, enjoying classes cancelled due to an "Act of God," play in the snow near Glen Arden Elementary School in Asheville.

Fire In the Sky *(top)*

MELISSA JO RICHART
NIKON N60
KODAK GOLD 100
F4

New Year fireworks light up the vista
seen from Town Mountain as
Asheville's *Light Up Your Holidays*
lights up the downtown below.

Fair View *(bottom)*

FRED BARKLEY
FUJI DISCOVERY
FUJI 100
AUTO

Seen from a home in Fairview, west of
Asheville, the winter sun goes down in
a blaze of red and orange.

Town Mountain

MELISSA JO RICHART
NIKON N60
KODAK GOLD 100
F8

The best seat in the city to watch
Asheville light up at night is Town
Mountain, on the northwest side of
Asheville. Over Town Mountain
Road, travellers can see the lights of
the neighboring towns twinkle in
the distance.

Winter Light

TIM BARNWELL
CANON F1 WITH 50MM LENS
FUJICHROME 100
F11

"Morning moved like a pearl-gray tide
across the fields and up the hill-flanks,
flowing rapidly into the soluble dark…"
–Thomas Wolfe, *Look Homeward,
Angel.*

First Snow *(top)*

ALYCE KASM PATRICK
PENTAX ZX-10
KODAK ROYAL 100
AUTO

The streets of Asheville are very quiet after a snowfall. The residents of Kimberly Street in North Asheville seem to have opted to stay warm indoors.

Over the River and Through the Woods *(bottom)*

KAREN L. STITELER
NIKON FM
KODAK 100
F22

Big Laurel Road in Marshall in Madison County, 30 miles northwest of Asheville, is still an isolated, rugged land populated by rugged individualists that define the region. Its winter snowfalls, statistically heavier than the rest of Western North Carolina, seem to suspend this mountain town in time.